World of Mammals

Walruses

by Connie Colwell Miller

Consultant:
Jaime R. Alvarado Bremer, PhD
Departments of Marine Biology and Wildlife and Fisheries Sciences
Texas A&M University
Galveston, Texas

Capstone press
Mankato, Minnesota

Bridgestone Books are published by Capstone Press,
151 Good Counsel Drive, P.O. Box 669, Mankato, Minnesota 56002.
www.capstonepress.com

Library of Congress Cataloging-in-Publication Data
Miller, Connie Colwell, 1976–
    Walruses / by Connie Colwell Miller.
        p. cm.—(Bridgestone Books. World of mammals)
    Summary: "A brief introduction to walruses, discussing their
characteristics, habitat, life cycle, and predators. Includes a range map,
life cycle illustration, and amazing facts"—Provided by publisher.
    Includes bibliographical references and index.
    ISBN 0-7368-4313-2 (hardcover)
    1. Walrus—Juvenile literature. I. Title. II. Series: World of mammals.
QL737.P62M55 2006
599.79'9—dc22   2004028440

Editorial Credits

Shari Joffe, editor; Molly Nei, set designer; Biner Design, book designer; Patricia Rasch, illustrator;
    Kelly Garvin, photo researcher; Scott Thoms, photo editor

Photo Credits

Bruce Coleman Inc./Len Rue Jr., 4
Corbis/Dan Guravich, 18
Digital Vision Ltd./Joel Simon, cover
Getty Images Inc./National Geographic/Norbert Rosing, 16
Minden Pictures/Foto Natura/Rinie Van Muers, 10
Seapics.com/Goran Ehlme, 12
SuperStock, Inc/Superstock, 6
Tom & Pat Leeson, 1, 20

1 2 3 4 5 6 10 09 08 07 06 05

Table of Contents

Walruses 5

What Walruses Look Like 7

Walruses in the World 9

Walrus Habitats 11

What Walruses Eat 13

Producing Young 15

Growing Up 17

Dangers to Walruses 19

Amazing Facts about Walruses 21

Glossary 22

Read More 23

Internet Sites 23

Index 24

Walruses

The walrus is an Arctic animal known for its huge body and long tusks. The tusks are actually strong, extra-long teeth. A walrus can pull itself out of the ocean with its tusks.

Walruses are sea **mammals**. Like land mammals, walruses have backbones and are **warm-blooded**.

Walruses are related to seals and sea lions. All three of these mammals have front and back flippers and eat meat. They live mainly in water but also spend time on land.

◄ A walrus's tusks continue to grow throughout the walrus's life.

What Walruses Look Like

Walruses look like very large seals. They can weigh up to 4,200 pounds (1,905 kilograms). They may be as long as 12 feet (3.6 meters).

Walruses have small heads and thick necks. Their tusks can be as long as 39 inches (99 centimeters). Male walruses usually have the longest tusks.

A walrus uses its front and back flippers to swim. It also uses its front flippers to pull itself up onto land and ice. This movement is called hauling out.

◄ Walruses have thick, reddish skin covered with short hairs.

Walrus Range Map

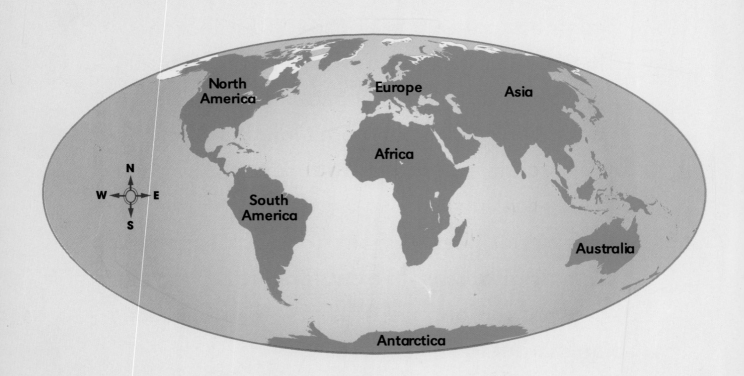

Where Walruses Live

Walruses in the World

Two kinds of walruses live in the world. Both live in the Arctic. Pacific walruses live in the North Pacific and Arctic Oceans. Atlantic walruses live in the North Atlantic Ocean near Canada and Greenland. Pacific walruses are bigger than Atlantic walruses. They also have longer tusks.

Walruses live in large groups called herds. Pacific walrus herds **migrate** south in the winter to the Bering Sea. They swim back north in the spring.

Walrus Habitats

Walruses live in icy water. They have a thick layer of fat called **blubber** under their skin. Blubber keeps walruses warm in cold water.

Walruses find food on the ocean bottom, so they usually stay in shallow water. They spend about one fifth of their time out of the water. They rest on floating chunks of ice called **floes**. Herds of walruses come ashore on small rocky islands when the ice melts in summer.

◄ Walruses live in shallow water near ice or land.

What Walruses Eat

Walruses eat mainly clams. Walruses find clams by diving to the bottom of the sea. They use their thick whiskers to feel along the sea floor and stir up clams. With their mouths, walruses suck the clams out of their shells.

Walruses also eat fish, worms, and other small sea animals. They do not chew their food. Instead, they swallow it whole.

◄ An Atlantic walrus searches for clams on the ocean bottom.

The Life Cycle of a Walrus

Newborn calf

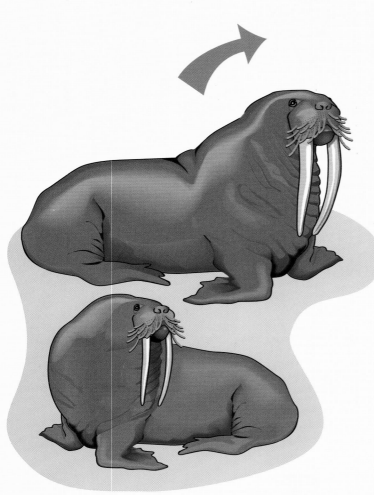
Adult male
and female

1-year-old

14

Producing Young

Walruses usually **mate** in the winter or early spring. They find their mating partners on land or ice. Male walruses make loud noises to get females to come near. Males sometimes fight with each other over females. The male with the largest tusks usually wins the fight. The male and female walruses then go into the water to mate.

A walrus calf is born about 15 months later. Walrus calves are born on the ice, usually in spring.

Growing Up

Newborn walruses look like adult walruses, but smaller. They weigh 100 to 165 pounds (45 to 75 kilograms). They are about 4 feet (1.2 meters) long.

A walrus calf drinks milk from its mother for up to two years. Walrus calves begin to eat food when they are about six months old. They stay close to their mothers for about two years.

◀ Walrus mothers take good care of their calves.

Dangers to Walruses

Walruses have few **predators**. Polar bears and killer whales sometimes kill young or weak walruses.

People are the greatest danger to walruses. Native Arctic peoples have hunted walruses for thousands of years. They need walrus meat and skin for food and clothing. In the 1600s, other people began hunting walruses for their tusks. Over time, too many walruses were killed.

Today, only native peoples are allowed to hunt walruses. These limits will help walruses continue to live on earth.

◄ Native Arctic peoples are allowed to hunt walruses because they depend on them for survival.

Amazing Facts about Walruses

- A walrus herd may have as many as 2,000 members.
- A walrus can eat 6,000 clams in one meal.
- Walrus calves sometimes ride on their mothers' backs.
- A walrus's color fades when the walrus goes underwater. Blood moves from the walrus's skin to its organs to keep the walrus warm.
- Walruses can sleep in the water. They poke their heads above the surface so they can breathe.

◄ A huge herd of Pacific walruses crowds onto an Alaskan shoreline.

Glossary

blubber (BLUH-bur)—the thick fat under the skin of a walrus

floe (FLOW)—large chunk of floating ice

mammal (MAM-uhl)—a warm-blooded animal that has a backbone; female mammals feed milk to their young.

mate (MAYT)—to join together to produce young

migrate (MYE-grate)—to move from one area to another

predator (PRED-uh-tur)—an animal that hunts other animals for food

warm-blooded (warm-BLUHD-id)—having a body temperature that stays the same

Read More

Murray, Julie. *Walruses.* A Buddy Book. Edina, Minn.: Abdo Publishing, 2003.

Rotter, Charles. *Walruses.* Naturebooks. Chanhassen, Minn.: Child's World, 2001.

Internet Sites

FactHound offers a safe, fun way to find Internet sites related to this book. All of the sites on FactHound have been researched by our staff.

Here's how:
1. Visit *www.facthound.com*
2. Type in this special code **0736843132** for age-appropriate sites. Or enter a search word related to this book for a more general search.
3. Click on the **Fetch It** button.

FactHound will fetch the best sites for you!

Index

backbone, 5
blubber, 11
body, 5, 7

dangers, 19

eating, 5, 13, 17, 21

flippers, 5, 7
floes, 11
food, 5, 11, 13, 17, 21

habitat, 5, 9, 11
hauling out, 7
heads, 7, 21
herds, 9, 11, 21

mammals, 5
mating, 15
migrating, 9
milk, 17
mouths, 13

necks, 7

people, 19
predators, 19

range, 9

size, 7, 9, 17
skin, 7, 11, 19, 21

teeth, 5
tusks, 5, 7, 9, 15, 17, 19

warm-blooded, 5
whiskers, 13

young, 15, 17, 19, 21